The SAVIOUR SENSITIVE CHURCH

Understanding and Avoiding
Post-Modernism and the
Seeker-Sensitive Church Movement

DR. PAUL CHAPPELL

DR. JOHN GOETSCH

Striving Together Publications
4020 E. Lancaster Blvd.
Lancaster, CA 93535
(800) 201-7748

Cover design by Jeremy Lofgren
Layout by Craig Parker
Typed by Julie Jenkins, Amy Houk, and Melanie Anderson
Compiled and edited by Cary Schmidt

Table of Contents

Dedication

This text is dedicated to the Lancaster Baptist Church family and the West Coast Baptist College student body. May God continue to give us His grace as we endeavor to be a Saviour-sensitive church training Saviour-sensitive spiritual leaders for the next generation of Christianity.

Forward

The following pages were developed from messages delivered at the Spiritual Leadership Conference at Lancaster Baptist Church in July 2004. Many Bible-believing Christians today are sensing the dramatic changes in the philosophy and practice of the modern church.

This book is divided into three parts. The first part—post modernism—gives biblical insight into the "root" problem of the culture at large, and the "church" culture in particular. The second section will contrast the characteristics of a Saviour-sensitive church to those of the seeker-sensitive philosophy. The third—the Saviour-sensitive church—explores the practical application of God's definition of a local church. These pages will expose the ungodly thinking that has taken hold in modern day Christendom and then challenge you to uphold a biblical model for ministry.

The first portion of this text was written by Dr. John Goetsch, the Executive Vice President of West Coast Baptist College. He has a passion for God and for revival. His life is dedicated to training young preachers and challenging God's people to develop a greater heart for God.

May God bless you as you read this book and may you renew your commitment to the absolute truth of the Word of God and the holiness of His church.

Dr. Paul Chappell
Pastor
Lancaster Baptist Church
Lancaster, CA

Introduction

The booklet you hold in your hands is written from hearts of concern and with a great desire to challenge pastors and church members across America to maintain a passionate sensitivity for Christ and His will in the church. The principles in this booklet are not based on a depressed longing for the "good ole days." Our desire is to speak the truth in love and, by the grace of God, challenge and edify the reader to be discerning in these days of ministry.

Many young pastors are looking at the fruit of so called "mega churches" and, because they desire to grow numerically and be in line with our success-oriented society, they are failing to look below the surface and see the "root systems" of the ministries with which they are enamored. A magazine recently reported a study by the University of Chicago that stated: "The proportion of adult Americans calling themselves Protestants, a steady 63% for decades, fell subtly to 52% in the last ten years."[1] It went on to state that for the first time, perhaps as early as 2005, America will no longer have a Protestant majority.

Though Baptists are not Protestant, it is interesting to note, the author of the article gave explanations for the decline of Protestantism. The explanation stated, "Mainline churches did not require enough commitment, theologically or evangelistically, from congregants." Even the Southern Baptist Convention has conceded a drop-off in Sunday school enrollment. It also is interesting to note that many of today's evangelical, and even some so-called fundamental churches, are embarking on a seeker-sensitive quest that strongly embraces a philosophy requiring less commitment "theologically and evangelistically."

We believe that, even as the mainline denominations of America are trending downward in their effectiveness and theological integrity, the churches of the seeker-sensitive movement will see similar results in the years to come.

This dilemma presents a great challenge for today's fundamental, Bible-believing pastor. As we continue to require commitment, "theologically and evangelistically,"

1.David Van Biema, *Roll Over, Martin Luther*, Time Magazine, August 16, 2004.

we will run the risk of being called "overbearing, legalistic, and uncaring." On the other hand, history is showing that churches requiring little commitment, "theologically and evangelistically," are dying on the vine all across America. In the eyes of reason, this presents a no-win situation. Fortunately, with eyes of faith we can interpret the facts quite differently!

We believe it would be far better for today's Christian leaders to stay true to God's unchanging Word and leave the numerical results completely up to Him. We believe that there is a great need for pastors and spiritual leaders across our nation to stop following cultural indicators and the whims of men. We still believe that the truth of God changes lives and that the work of the local church is one of supernatural origin and result! In other words, a true church cannot be grown to health and vitality apart from the divine touch of God and His eternal, unchanging Word. The local church is God's work, and while there is a vast movement sweeping churches into compromise, through these pages we hope to challenge you to stand strong and stay true to God's plan.

We must challenge God's people to remain committed and we must lead them by example. We must uphold commitment to doctrine, to truth, to godly living, and to personal soulwinning. Then we must leave the results up to God.

In this day when churches are constantly looking for a new method, a new movie, or the next "seeker-sensitive fad," we believe God is looking for renewed men and women, who have a fresh anointing from Him, a passion for Him, and a passion for revival.

Thank you for reading. It is our prayer that God will use this material to strengthen you and your church as you run your race for the Lord Jesus Christ.

PART ONE

Post-Modernism

by Dr. John Goetsch

CHAPTER ONE

Post-Modernism

*I charge thee therefore before God, and the Lord
Jesus Christ, who shall judge the quick and the
dead at his appearing and his kingdom; Preach
the word; be instant in season, out of season;
reprove, rebuke, exhort with all longsuffering and
doctrine. For the time will come when they will
not endure sound doctrine; but after their own
lusts shall they heap to themselves teachers, having
itching ears; And they shall turn away their ears
from the truth, and shall be turned unto fables.
But watch thou in all things, endure afflictions,
do the work of an evangelist, make full proof of
thy ministry.* II Timothy 4:1–5

Several years ago I was driving late at night, on my way to
a meeting, and trying to stay awake. My normal practice

3

at a particularly drowsy stage is to begin scanning radio stations to find something that makes me angry. As I did this, I stumbled across an interview with a PhD from Harvard. This man was a math professor. I don't really recall the setting of the interview or why he was being interviewed, but at one point this man said, "If a child says, 'two plus two equals five,' we cannot tell that child that he is wrong."

The host said, "Now wait a minute. Did I hear you correctly? You just said if a child says, 'two plus two equals five,' we cannot tell the child that he is wrong?"

The professor replied, "Absolutely. We must not tell the child that his answer is wrong."

The interviewer said, "But, he is wrong."

"Well, no," he said, "he may be wrong to you, but to him that is the right answer."

At the time, I laughed at this crackpot PhD from Harvard, but I have since discovered that this is not just an isolated way of thinking. This way of thinking is called post-modernism and it has now overtaken modernism as the prevailing mode of thought that is influencing our culture. This way of thinking is literally casting a dark shadow over both reason and scientific method in our culture today.

By definition, post-modernism asserts that external absolute truth—that is a truth that is true for all people in all places at all times—cannot be known through reason or science because truth is non-existent or unattainable.

Several years ago, Allen Bloom stated in his book *The Closing of the American Mind*:

> "There is one thing of which a professor can be absolutely certain—almost every student entering the university believes or says they believe that truth is relative. They are unified only in their relativism and in their allegiance to equality. The danger they have been taught to fear from absolutism is not error, but intolerance. Relativism is necessary to openness and this is the virtue, the only virtue, to which all primary education has dedicated itself for the past fifty years of inculcating."[1]

You see, in the 1960s we had this saying, "Do your own thing." To most of us who grew up in that era this thinking was kind of a passing trend. It seemed to be just another fad. The world was quickly becoming a place where people were "doing their own thing." It was almost funny, at the time. However, this philosophy, though somewhat of a passing fad outwardly, went a lot deeper and developed into a *"think* your own thing" philosophy.

Shortly thereafter we were introduced to "values clarification"—a thinking that assured people that all moral values are relative and, therefore, acceptable. The outgrowth of this is epistemological relativity, which is the idea that people can only know truth from their own experiences, which now makes all truth relative. In this

1. Allen Bloom, *The Closing of the American Mind*, (New York: Simon & Schuster, Inc., 1988).

relativistic way of thinking, we can still talk about truth, but we can only talk about what is true for *you* and what is true for *me*.

How many times in the past six months have you met people at a doorstep—someone you were witnessing to–who were open to what you had to say only with surface interest? They were willing, to some degree, to listen to your religion, your thoughts, and what you might tell them from the Bible. Then they said, "Well, that's what *you* believe, but it's not what *I* believe." They justify themselves to be just as right as you are, and on their way to Heaven just as you say you are. Their justification is that there is no absolute truth. In other words, what is true for you, may not be true for me.

Suddenly, what has happened in the 21st century is that truth, with a capital T, which is absolute truth, has been replaced with truth, with a small t, which stands for relative truth.

Therefore, while society and culture are still talking about truth, we are talking about two different kinds of truth. When Bible-believing Christians come together around the Word of God to talk about truth, we had better be talking about absolute truth—capital T truth—truth that does not change and is the same for every person, in every place, in every situation, throughout every generation.

Yet, when the world and culture talk about truth today they are not talking about capital T truth. The world no longer believes in absolute, unchanging truth.

This moral relativity has resulted in chaos and confusion, because when there are no absolutes, no one can determine right from wrong. This is not the thinking of America's forefathers, nor is it the thinking of Christians throughout the ages! Gradually, this relativity has led to a tolerance of any and all ways of thinking—except any thinking that declares or believes in absolute Truth. You see, the only thing that post-modern culture is intolerant of is absolute Truth.

For instance, we are told not speak out against same-sex marriages and other sins which the Bible clearly condemns, because, "Hey, what you believe is true for you, but what someone else believes is truth for them—they have their rights."

I believe that fundamental Baptist leadership is at a crossroads. We stand at a critical fork in the road which has immense implications for generations to come; and we must decide if we are going to follow "designer truth" or "discovered truth." Will we choose a relativistic approach to Christianity? Will the post-modern thought enter into our pulpits and Sunday school classrooms? Or will we take our stand against culture—will we hold fast to absolute Truth? Friend, you stand at this crossroad and you must decide today, which of the two kinds of truth you will follow—capital *T* truth or small *t* truth.

Before we go further allow me to insert, I am not discouraged or pessimistic about where we are in this culture. I am not a fatalist. Jesus looked at the multitudes, in Matthew 9, and He saw them as sheep without a shepherd.

> And Jesus went about all the cities and villages, teaching in their synagogues, and preaching the gospel of the kingdom, and healing every sickness and every disease among the people. But when he saw the multitudes, he was moved with compassion on them, because they fainted, and were scattered abroad, as sheep having no shepherd. Then saith he unto his disciples, The harvest truly is plenteous, but the labourers are few; Pray ye therefore the Lord of the harvest, that he will send forth labourers into his harvest.
> Matthew 9:35–38

God likens people to sheep. They will follow leadership and many of God's people today are following leaders that are leading them into relative truth. Even so called "Christian" leaders are coming along with small **t** truth. They are looking for someone to lead. As spiritual leaders, we have the privilege of going out into this world, finding those sheep that are scattered abroad, and leading them to God and to the absolute, unchanging Truth of His Word.

Sadly, in the book of Ezekiel chapter 34 God said, "My *sheep wandered through all the mountains, and upon every high hill: yea, my flock was scattered upon all the face of the earth, and none did search or seek after them.*"

In your community and around the world today, people are scattered upon every hill—confused, dazed, wounded, weary, bombarded with all kinds of paraphernalia and the filth of the world. All of this leaves them in an unsettled state. It is time for God's men and women to rise to the task and be spiritual leaders. It is time for us to stand courageously against the relative, post-modern thought that has overtaken our culture and that is creeping into our churches as well. It is time for us to shoulder the mantle of truth, as spiritual shepherds, leading God's people back to the discovered truth, rather than allowing the Devil's hirelings to lead them after designer truth.

> *All we like sheep have gone astray; we have turned every one to his own way...* Isaiah 53:6

> *For the pastors are become brutish, and have not sought the LORD: therefore they shall not prosper, and all their flocks shall be scattered.* Jeremiah 10:21

> *Woe be unto the pastors that destroy and scatter the sheep of my pasture! saith the LORD.* Jeremiah 23:1

CHAPTER TWO

Designer Truth

In II Timothy 4 Paul is nearing his death and he is about to hand off the baton to the next generation of preachers. This passage exposes some stark contrasts between designer truth and discovered truth as Paul warns Timothy of the very thinking that we face in modern day Christendom. Look at this passage again:

> *I charge thee therefore before God, and the Lord Jesus Christ, who shall judge the quick and the dead at his appearing and his kingdom; Preach the word; be instant in season, out of season; reprove, rebuke, exhort with all longsuffering and doctrine. For the time will come when they will not endure sound doctrine; but after their own lusts shall they heap to themselves teachers, having*

itching ears; And they shall turn away their ears from the truth, and shall be turned unto fables. But watch thou in all things, endure afflictions, do the work of an evangelist, make full proof of thy ministry. II Timothy 4:1–5

Designer Truth Is Evolving Truth

Designer truth is the truth with a small **t**. This is relative truth which attempts to appeal to everybody, all the time. This truth speaks out of both sides of its mouth, if you please. Designer truth is an evolving truth that morphs and changes with the whims of society.

Look at verse three where Paul says, *"For the time will come when they will not endure sound doctrine;"* Paul is saying that people are going to look for change. They are not going to know why they want change, but they want change and they will not endure what is already in place. They will not put up with what is already established. They will be attracted to that which is new, to that which is designed rather than discovered. Paul is warning Timothy that people are not always going to follow this absolute truth. They are going to be enamored with something that is flexible to the whims of man.

Today, the post-modernist says, "Reason and science are fogged and contaminated by world views, prejudices, environment and upbringing—all of which render it undependable as an instrument for grasping absolute truth. Therefore, the idea of truth is created rather than discovered."

What they are telling us today is that what you believe as absolute truth has been clouded by your background, your religious teaching, and those who have influenced you in a wrong way, namely God. They say you are too fogged up in your mind to really know what absolute truth is. Truth, they say, is not something that can be discovered, but rather created as we go–and something that is different for every person depending upon their individual experiences.

By the way, Romans 1:18 says, *"For the wrath of God is revealed from heaven against all ungodliness and unrighteousness of men, who hold the truth in unrighteousness;"* Romans 1:25 continues to say, *"Who changed the truth of God into a lie, and worshipped and served the creature more than the Creator, who is blessed for ever. Amen."* God is on top of this! It isn't catching Him by surprise! God knew exactly where we were headed in the 21st century. He knew we were going to try to change truth and this is exactly what Paul is warning about here. People will turn away from absolute truth in search of something that is evolving.

In our government, an example of this would be that the self-evident truths, about which our forefathers spoke as they worded the Constitution and the Bill of Rights, are apparently no longer self-evident since truth cannot possibly be self-evident—it is always being discovered differently by every individual.

Spiritually, there are other examples. In fact, when you step back and look at this it is laughable. Today, we see the growth of the neo-evangelical movement— neo meaning "new." In other words, we desire new evangelicalism instead of the old-time evangelicalism. Apparently whatever was represented by the "old evangelicalism" has evolved or changed or become outdated.

Worse yet, we now want a *new* King James Bible, or a *new* International Version or a *new* American Standard. This post-modern concept has completely overtaken even our view of God's Word.

Christians today want evolving truth—truth that is changing. You might find it hard to get a neo-evangelical to admit this, but at the root, this is clearly the case. Friend, this is ridiculous! Who wants truth that changes?

I asked a friend in high school, "What happened to Saint Christopher? He used to be on your rearview mirror?"

He replied, "Oh, we decided he's not a saint anymore."

Another change while I was in high school was "Hey, you can eat meat on Fridays now. No more fish sticks on Fridays for lunch."

I ask you again, "Who wants truth that changes?"

By the way, do you suppose the movie theatre is less of a threat to your congregation today than it was in Billy Sunday's day? Then, why in the world are so-called fundamental Baptist preachers becoming more and more tolerant of Hollywood? Why are some even taking their congregations to the theatre to see supposed "Christian" movies?

Does CCM music have more Scripture than the hymns of Fanny Crosby and Isaac Watts? Do the sounds and musical styles of modern day pop bands in churches really help us to be filled with the Holy Spirit as Ephesians 5 teaches us to be concerning "psalms and hymns and spiritual songs?"

> *"And be not drunk with wine, wherein is excess; but be filled with the Spirit; Speaking to yourselves in psalms and hymns and spiritual songs, singing and making melody in your heart to the Lord; Giving thanks always for all things unto God and the Father in the name of our Lord Jesus Christ;"* Ephesians 5:18–20

Friend, the Bible is the same today as it was the day God gave it to us! Nothing has changed, yet designer truth is always evolving truth. Second Timothy 3:7 refers to it this way, *"Ever learning, and never able to come to the knowledge of the truth."*

Designer Truth Is Experiential Truth

God says in II Timothy 4:3, *"For the time will come when they will not endure sound doctrine;* **but after their own lusts***..."*—experiential truth.

Today's culture trusts its selfish lusts rather than God's sovereign love. Every man does what is right in his own eyes. Proverbs 14:12, *"There is a way which seemeth right unto a man, but the end thereof are the ways of death.*

There is a way that seemeth right unto a man and we are strongly heading that direction in our churches today.

> *Knowing this first, that there shall come in the last days scoffers, walking after their own lusts, And saying, Where is the promise of his coming? for since the fathers fell asleep, all things continue as they were from the beginning of the creation. For this they willingly are ignorant of, that by the word of God the heavens were of old, and the earth standing out of the water and in the water: Whereby the world that then was, being overflowed with water, perished: But the heavens and the earth, which are now, by the same word are kept in store, reserved unto fire against the day of judgment and perdition of ungodly men.*
> II Peter 3:3–7

Peter warned that there would be those who would scoff at the Bible, God, and Truth. Why do they scoff at the Bible? Because they do not think it is true? No, they know it is true.

In Romans 1, God has revealed Himself to every man who has walked this planet.

> *For the wrath of God is revealed from heaven against all ungodliness and unrighteousness of men, who hold the truth in unrighteousness; Because that which may be known of God is manifest in them; for God hath shewed it unto them. For the invisible things of him from the creation of the world are clearly seen, being*

> *understood by the things that are made, even*
> *his eternal power and Godhead; so that they are*
> *without excuse.* Romans 1:18–20

God does not believe in atheists. Man does not scoff at the Bible because he does not think there is a God or because he does not think it is true. Romans 2 tells us that God has written it on man's heart.

> *For when the Gentiles, which have not the law, do*
> *by nature the things contained in the law, these,*
> *having not the law, are a law unto themselves:*
> *Which shew the work of the law written in their*
> *hearts, their conscience also bearing witness, and*
> *their thoughts the mean while accusing or else*
> *excusing one another.* Romans 2:14–15

Man scoffs at the Bible because he is walking after his own lusts. "*And this is the condemnation, that light is come into the world, and men loved darkness rather than light, because their deeds were evil. For every one that doeth evil hateth the light, neither cometh to the light, lest his deeds should be reproved*" (John 3:19–20).

Where the rubber meets the road is that man does not want to accept absolute truth because he does not want to change his ways. Man wants experiential truth. You see, post-modernism is based on the premise that truth is created rather than discovered. The post-modernist's personal experiences define their needs and shape their answers to those needs. In spite of their belief that we cannot really know the truth, they understand that all individuals must have some sort of working philosophy as a framework for their thoughts and values. Therefore, they must create their own truths based on what works for them.

This thinking lead to pragmatism–a philosophical way of creating truth based on experience or based upon "what works." In other words, if it feels good, do it.

Sadly, this is where the seeker-sensitive church idea originates. This pragmatic view leads churches to attempt to do God's work in whatever way feels good—whatever way appears to "work the best"—whatever way is the most acceptable to the unchurched. These churches say, "We have to have some truth so let's just base our truths on what people want. We will give them what they want and what they want to experience."

Pastors and church growth experts go to great lengths to study, understand, and cater their churches and their sermons to the ever changing whims of the masses rather than to the clear, absolute truth of God's unchanging Word! There is no end to this slippery slope because the whims of the masses are constantly changing. The community surveys, the Christian pop music revolution, the continually evolving truth of various Bible-versions will produce an unending cycle of redesigned and repackaged truth, which are always attempting to please people and getting further and further from God's revealed Word.

By the way, if a pastor is afraid to preach a Bible-based truth in church because he is afraid someone is going to leave, he is just as seeker-sensitive as those who cater to the whims of secular culture. God has commanded us to teach and preach the whole counsel of God.

> *Wherefore I take you to record this day, that I am pure from the blood of all men. For I have not shunned to declare unto you all the counsel of God. Take heed therefore unto yourselves, and to all the flock, over the which the Holy Ghost hath made you overseers, to feed the church of God, which he hath purchased with his own blood.*
> Acts 20:26–28

We have seen that designer truth is evolving truth and experiential truth, but I want you to see a third quality of designer truth.

Designer Truth Is Eclectic Truth

Second Timothy 4:3 says, *For the time will come when they will not endure sound doctrine; but after their own lusts shall they heap to themselves **teachers.***" Notice the plurality of authority. Not one undershepherd or one absolute God, but many teachers and instructors. Not one Bible of absolute truth, but as many versions as you want.

Someone recently gave me an article from the Internet. It was about a new Bible. This particular version might as well have been called the "fornicators version." It changed I Corinthians 7 to speak graphically about lust. It gave nicknames to the characters in the Bible, like changing Peter to Rocky. They gave Jesus another name, which I will not even mention. They interpret the

I Corinthians 7 passage as saying, "God doesn't want you to lust so go grab somebody." These are the exact words. Where does this sort of thinking stop? Where do all these versions stop? How far is too far?

You see with every new generation of Christians there is a new generation of truth—a revised, updated, better version. With every revised version we move farther and farther from God's truth and closer and closer to apostasy.

As Christians, we must have an absolute authority. We must have absolute truth. Our truth cannot be a gathering of our favorites wordings from dozens of different texts or versions. This is designer truth—eclectic—made up of the preferred stylings from multiple sources.

Designer truth says that we can have many Bibles, a plurality of elders in the church, committees to decide what to do (so nothing will get done!). Ultimately this leads to many gods and many sources of truth. You can be your own god. If there is more than one authority for truth, you can become your own authority.

In a nutshell, post-modernism says, "If it is true for you, then it is as true as it needs to be and no one has the right to question what you have chosen as truth for yourself."

Designer Truth Is Elevated Truth

Fourthly, designer truth becomes elevated truth. Second Timothy 4:4 states: *"And they shall turn away their ears from the truth, and shall be turned unto fables."* The word *fables* simply means "false, fictitious, ludicrous." At this point in the decline, truth with a little *t* becomes desired above truth with a capital *T,* and designer truth becomes the elevated truth. As Romans 1:21–22 teaches us, *"Because that, when they knew God, they glorified him not as God, neither were thankful; but became vain in their imaginations, and their foolish heart was darkened. Professing themselves to be wise, they became fools,"*

Isaiah 47:10 says, *"For thou hast trusted in thy wickedness: thou hast said, None seeth me. Thy wisdom and thy knowledge, it hath perverted thee; and thou hast said in thine heart, I am, and none else beside me."*

Friend, the term "I Am" is reserved for one Person, and it is not you or me. Yet, today we have become our own gods and post-modernism borders on new-age mysticism, which says "If you believe something strongly enough, the universe, or God, will endorse it." New agers believe that there is something inherently powerful in the nature of a strongly held belief that moves the powers that be to bring reality into alignment with your belief.

As a pastor, you have probably seen this in your own ministry. People can sit in your office, living in sin, justify it, and convince themselves that God has endorsed it. It is like telling your children there is a Santa Claus, and then on Christmas morning, making sure there are presents under the tree to endorse what they believe. In this case the fantasy—the fable—becomes the preferred belief, and the believer will go to great lengths to bring reality and rationale into line with the fable.

The following passages give reference to the fact that men will be bent upon rejecting God's truth. The sad reality is that this practice is common even in many churches which claim the name of Christ.

> *But if thine heart turn away, so that thou wilt not hear, but shalt be drawn away, and worship other gods, and serve them.* Deuteronomy 30:17

> *He that turneth away his ear from hearing the law, even his prayer shall be abomination.* Proverbs 28:9

> *His watchmen are blind: they are all ignorant, they are all dumb dogs, they cannot bark; sleeping, lying down, loving to slumber. Yea, they are greedy dogs which can never have enough, and they are shepherds that cannot understand: they all look to their own way, every one for his gain, from his quarter. Come ye, say they, I will fetch wine, and we will fill ourselves with strong drink; and to morrow shall be as this day, and much more abundant.* Isaiah 56:10–12

> *The prophets prophesy falsely, and the priests bear rule by their means; and my people love to have it so: and what will ye do in the end thereof?* Jeremiah 5:31

> *Son of man, thou dwellest in the midst of a rebellious house, which have eyes to see, and see not; they have ears to hear, and hear not: for they are a rebellious house.* Ezekiel 12:2

CHAPTER THREE

Discovered Truth

Now, let's compare this small *t* truth, designer truth, to the capital *T* truth, which is discovered truth—something that is already here. Discovered truth is something that stands outside the realm of my experience or intellect or anyone else's—something that stands neutral and unchanging apart from me or anything that I am.

Discovered Truth Is Eternal Truth

In II Timothy 4:1, Paul begins this passage by saying, "*I charge thee therefore before God, and the Lord Jesus Christ, who shall judge the quick and the dead at his appearing and his kingdom.*" Contrasted to evolving truth, discovered truth is an eternal truth. The reason truth is eternal is because the Author of that truth is eternal. *"For I am the LORD, I change not;"* (Malachi 3:6a)

"God is not a man, that he should lie; neither the son of man, that he should repent: hath he said, and shall he not do it? or hath he spoken, and shall he not make it good?" (Numbers 23:19) *"Every good gift and every perfect gift is from above, and cometh down from the Father of lights, with whom is no variableness, neither shadow of turning."* (James 1:17) God's truth does not change with the times. It is not culturally relative. It is not pragmatic. It is eternal truth because God Himself is eternal and unchanging.

> *Of old hast thou laid the foundation of the earth: and the heavens are the work of thy hands. They shall perish, but thou shalt endure: yea, all of them shall wax old like a garment; as a vesture shalt thou change them, and they shall be changed: But thou art the same, and thy years shall have no end.* Psalms 102:25–27

Discovered Truth Is Established Truth

Paul says in verse two, *"Preach the word."* He is commanding Timothy to preach what is already established. Preach what God has already given. You cannot improve on *"Thus saith the Lord."*

In many pulpits today, the Scripture reference has about as much to do with the sermon as the National Anthem has to do with a football game! It gets the message started and we never hear from it again! Preacher, you would be better off to get what you have to say out of the way in the first few seconds of your message, and then just read the Bible for the remainder of your pulpit time. It is God's Word—God's eternal, unchanging truth that has an eternal, living, powerful impact upon the hearts of men.

> *For the word of God is quick, and powerful, and sharper than any twoedged sword, piercing even to the dividing asunder of soul and spirit, and of the joints and marrow, and is a discerner of the thoughts and intents of the heart. Neither is there any creature that is not manifest in his sight: but all things are naked and opened unto the eyes of him with whom we have to do.* Hebrews 4:12–13

God's Word is established truth, based, as Paul says, on sound doctrine. Second Timothy 4:3, *"For the time will come when they will not endure sound doctrine;"* God's truth is outside and exists in authority above the realm of your experience. His truth is true even when it completely contradicts your personal experience.

Peter made this clear when he said in II Peter 1:16 *"For we have not followed cunningly devised fables, when we made known unto you the power and coming of our Lord Jesus Christ, but were eyewitnesses of his majesty."* In verses 19–21, he compares his eyewitness account to Scripture by saying,

> *We have also a more sure word of prophecy; whereunto ye do well that ye take heed, as unto a light that shineth in a dark place, until the day dawn, and the day star arise in your hearts:*

Knowing this first, that no prophecy of the scripture is of any private interpretation. For the prophecy came not in old time by the will of man: but holy men of God spake as they were moved by the Holy Ghost.

Quite literally, God's Truth—God's Word is so true and so eternal that it is should be the authority in your life even above personal experience!

You see, outside of us there is a God, Who has established truth. *"For ever, O LORD, thy word is settled in heaven."* (Psalms 119:89) If it is settled in Heaven, it is settled on earth, too!

Concerning thy testimonies, I have known of old that thou hast founded them for ever. Psalms 119:152

Heaven and earth shall pass away: but my words shall not pass away. Luke 21:33

And it is easier for heaven and earth to pass, than one tittle of the law to fail. Luke 16:17

The Scriptures cannot be broken!

Being born again, not of corruptible seed, but of incorruptible, by the word of God, which liveth and abideth for ever. For all flesh is as grass, and all the glory of man as the flower of grass. The grass withereth, and the flower thereof falleth away: But the word of the Lord endureth for ever. And this is the word which by the gospel is preached unto you. I Peter 1:23–25

It is established truth! *"Thus saith the Lord!"* The Bible stands and it will continue to stand forever!

Discovered Truth Is Examined Truth

In II Timothy 4:2 God says that His truth *"reproves, rebukes and exhorts."* These modern-day eclectic truth—designers examine their buffet of Bibles in their seminary cloisters. This is backwards! We need a generation of people who will let the absolute truth of *"thus saith the Lord"* examine *them!* One old preacher said it this way, "Quit studying your Bible; let your Bible study you!"

The context is not that you should literally quit studying your Bible, but rather that you should stop approaching is with an heir of superiority as though you must determine in your own wisdom what God has said. It's time that we give ourselves to God's Word in a spirit of humility and submission—truly allowing the living oracles of the eternal God to search our deepest hearts and pierce the innermost recesses of our beings! It's time we approach the Word of God with a spirit of submitted obedience—coming under God's final authority determined to be conformed to Christ and transformed by God's power.

Pastor, God is more interested in making a messenger than he is in you making messages. Someone said, "Preaching is making a message and delivering it." To which Bishop Quayle said, "No, that is not preaching at all. Preaching is God making a messenger and preaching that."

The living, unchanging Word of God must be given access to our hearts, because the heart of man is *"deceitful above all things and desperately wicked: who can know it?"* (Jeremiah 17:9) *"For the word of God is quick, and powerful, and sharper than any twoedged sword, piercing even to the dividing asunder of soul and spirit, and of the joints and marrow, and is a discerner of the thoughts and intents of the heart."* (Hebrews 4:12)

My friend, when you delve into God's Word with a heart of submission, it will uncover, reveal, bring to light what you are and what I am. We must be examined under its supernatural, microscopic power. We need an MRI of the Word of God in our lives to let it show us what we really are. *"All scripture is given by inspiration of God, and is profitable for doctrine, for reproof, for correction, for instruction in righteousness: that the man of God may be perfect, throughly furnished unto all good works."* (II Timothy 3:16–17) That is why Jeremiah said, *"The prophet that hath a dream, let him tell a dream; and he that hath my word, let him speak my word faithfully. What is the chaff to the wheat? saith the LORD. Is not my word like as a fire? saith the LORD; and like a hammer that breaketh the rock in pieces?"* (Jeremiah 23:28–29)

If your heart has become hard, let the Word of God smash that heart. Let it break your heart down into little pieces again, where God can put it back together for His glory. Let the fire of God's Word melt the ice in your heart, and get you on fire for the things of God.

A *new heart also will I give you, and a new spirit will I put within you: and I will take away the stony heart out of your flesh, and I will give you an heart of flesh. And I will put my spirit within you, and cause you to walk in my statutes, and ye shall keep my judgments, and do them.* Ezekiel 36:26–27

Discovered Truth Is Enduring Truth

In II Timothy 4:5 Paul says, "*But watch thou in all things, endure afflictions, do the work of an evangelist, make full proof of thy ministry.*" He is saying, "Timothy, one day you are going to be where I am—about ready to put your head on a chopping block. When you get there, you make sure that you stay by the stuff, because Truth is an enduring truth. Capital **T** truth, discovered truth, doesn't change."

One day, when it is all over, we are not going to stand before small **t** truth. We will stand before capital **T** truth! "*He that rejecteth me, and receiveth not my words, hath one that judgeth him: the word that I have spoken, the same shall judge him in the last day.*" (John 12:48) Regardless of what this culture says, one day the absolute Truth of God will examine our lives.

The captain of a ship looked out into the foggy distance and saw some faint lights directly in the path of the vessel. He ordered the signalman to send a message: "Altar your course ten degrees south."

A reply came back, "Alter your course ten degrees north." The captain was enraged. His command had been ignored. He sent a second message: "Alter your course ten degrees south. I am a captain."

A moment passed. A message returned: "Alter your course ten degrees north. I am seaman third class Jones." The captain was indignant. He could not believe what he had heard. He sent the third message: "Alter your course ten degrees south. I am a battleship."

The reply came: "Alter your course ten degrees north. I am a lighthouse."

Do not waste your time and money trying to tell God to altar His course. You will spend the rest of your life in ministry with your wheels spinning if you follow designer truth. Truth does not change. The Lighthouse still stands and will forever!

Two Churches in Contrast

by Dr. Paul Chappell

CHAPTER FOUR

Biblical Ministry vs. Man-Centered Ministry

Nearly two decades ago, my wife and I left a wonderful church in northern California and drove a Ryder moving van to northern Los Angeles County to begin working with a small group of people to re-establish the Lancaster Baptist Church. I vividly recall the first Saturday night in Lancaster, as Terrie and I sat in the living room of our two-bedroom apartment, and constructed the first church bulletin. There was not much to say about the activities of the church because there were very few to announce! I decided it would be an opportune time to list some of the distinctives of the church in the bulletin.

In the bulletin we stated that Lancaster Baptist Church was an independent, fundamental, Bible-believing, separated Baptist church. With a strong doctrinal position and a heart for souls, we began preaching the Word of God fervently, and sharing the Gospel passionately in our community.

After being at the church a few Sundays, I distinctively remember after a service a man saying to me, "You cannot build a church in Southern California this way. This type of preaching and the old-fashioned music will no longer work. Churches that are growing in California will only grow if they use rock 'n roll music and a less emphatic preaching style."

As a young, zealous (and probably somewhat insecure) pastor, I remember telling the man distinctly that the word "preach" in the New Testament involved a strong declaration of the truth and that the singing of the church has always included psalms, hymns and "spiritual" songs. I told him that there were several churches down the street from us who would probably be glad to accommodate his desire, but that we intended to hold to our position.

It is interesting to study the early New Testament churches. In the letters to the churches, I find that each one apparently had a different personality, as well as a different spiritual fervor. Some churches were noble to search the Scriptures. Others seemed to disregard the early admonitions of the apostles.

Few churches in the New Testament can be contrasted like the church of Laodicea and the church of Thessalonica. In Revelation chapters two and three, we see the Lord speaking to the seven literal churches of Asia Minor. Each of these churches also seems to be a type of the seven stages of church history. The last church, the church of Laodicea, is of interesting note for the discerning Christian.

A short study of the etymology of the word "laodicea" shows the meaning to be "the people's rights." The Laodicean church was the church of the people's rights. Revelation 3:14 indicates the church was referred to as, "the church of the Laodiceans" rather than "the church of Laodicea." It was, indeed, the people's church. The people's rights were pre-eminent. In many ways this was the first seeker-sensitive church in church history.

No God-fearing pastor would desire his church to reflect the characteristics of the Laodicean church. Yet slowly, and sometimes like a frog in the kettle, unknowingly, good churches are being affected by the poor and unbiblical philosophies being taught at many seminars today.

Even George Barna, a Christian pollster, recently said in an interview, "I am really concerned about complacency among our churches. We are the church of Laodicea. We think we are hot stuff. We think the world takes its cues from us. We think we are tight with God, but really we don't have a clue."[1]

The church at Thessalonica stands in stark contrast to the church of Laodicea. Thessalonica was located about one hundred miles from Philippi on the Egnation Highway. Though the apostle Paul had initially only been

---

1. *SBC Life Magazine*, June 2004 edition

there for a few weeks, the Holy Spirit moved mightily, as he proclaimed the Gospel in this strategic location.

In I Thessalonians 1:3, Paul later wrote to the church and said, *"Remembering without ceasing your work of faith, and labour of love, and patience of hope in our Lord Jesus Christ, in the sight of God and our Father;"*

Notice with me, some of the early characteristics of this church and of Paul's ministry at Thessalonica. In I Thessalonians chapters one and two, the apostle Paul is defending the integrity of his ministry at Thessalonica and defining the qualities of the Saviour-sensitive church.

A Church with Pure Motives

First of all, we learn that the church at Thessalonica was a church with pure motives.

> *For our exhortation was not of deceit, nor of uncleanness, nor in guile: But as we were allowed of God to be put in trust with the gospel, even so we speak; not as pleasing men, but God, which trieth our hearts. For neither at any time used we flattering words, as ye know, nor a cloke of covetousness; God is witness: Nor of men sought we glory, neither of you, nor yet of others, when we might have been burdensome, as the apostles of Christ.* I Thessalonians 2:3–6

We sense that, as Paul defends the integrity of the church at Thessalonica, he is aware that if his enemies could awaken distrust concerning him as a messenger, it would bring distrust to the message. Therefore, he very carefully shows us the motives of his ministry in that city.

He first reminded the Thessalonians that his ministry had not been a deceitful one, or a ministry "in guile." The temples at Thessalonica were definitely places of deceit. People attended a temple, perhaps desiring to draw closer to God, but in fact, the end result was the opposite.

In the same way, much of the philosophy of the seeker-sensitive movement is deceitful. Churches are telling people to come just as they are, and stay as they are! They play the world's music, tell the world's jokes, encourage people to continue the way they want to live and, generally, tell people that there is no need for outward change in the Christian life.

The deceitfulness of this is found in the scriptural admonition from Romans 12:2, which says, *"And be not conformed to this world: but be ye transformed by the renewing of your mind, that ye may prove what is that good, and acceptable, and perfect, will of God."* Furthermore, in II Corinthians 5:17, the apostle says, *"Therefore if any man be in Christ, he is a new creature: old things are passed away; behold, all things are become new."*

To attract a crowd to church by encouraging them to come just as they are and leave without any change is to practice a kind of Christianity foreign to the teaching of the Bible.

Secondly, the apostle Paul stated that he was not unclean in his ministry. Paul was a morally pure man. Paul stated that his ministry was not in guile. The word "guile" means "to bate or to snare." It speaks of using trickery or deceit.

When the term "new evangelicalism" was coined at Fuller Seminary by Harold Ockenga, his desire was to bring the modernists (deniers of the truth) together with the fundamentalists (believers of the truth) by encouraging them to compromise doctrinally. It was a movement of guile intended to bate or snare people together for the purpose of drawing a crowd. The seeds of this type of compromise are evident in many ecumenical gatherings today.

Essentially, the apostle is saying that the church at Thessalonica had integrity, as opposed to duplicity. It was evident that the Thessalonican believers assembled for the purpose of preaching the Gospel and giving Christ pre-eminence. In II Timothy 3:10, Paul said, *"But thou hast fully known my doctrine, manner of life, purpose, faith, longsuffering, charity, patience,"*

Years ago, the Lord called my dear friend, Dr. Curtis Hutson, home after a long battle with cancer. Dr. Hutson wrote me many letters in the final days of his life. One letter stated:

> "I don't know how much longer I have for this world. The doctor does not hold out much hope for me; however, life and death are in the hands of the Lord, not medical science.

> "I challenge you to take your place in the long line of independent, fundamental Baptists, who have stood for separation and soulwinning. I speak, now, especially of ecclesiastical separation. Hold that banner high until Jesus comes."

Dr. Hutson was admonishing and encouraging me to beware of deceitful gatherings that drop doctrinal distinctives for the purpose of gathering a crowd.

As Paul speaks of the motives of his ministry, we notice, secondly, that they were not man-centered.

> *But as we were allowed of God to be put in trust with the gospel, even so we speak; not as pleasing men, but God, which trieth our hearts. For neither at any time used we flattering words, as ye know, nor a cloke of covetousness; God is witness: Nor of men sought we glory, neither of you, nor yet of others, when we might have been burdensome, as the apostles of Christ.* I Thessalonians 2:4–6

The Laodicean churches of our day have unashamedly tailored their ministries after the desires of men. Seminars are given in which pastors are taught how to please men in the services.

I'm certainly not opposed to helping unregenerate men understand Bible words. I have challenged fundamental pastors in our day to make sure that our messages are clearly defined and easily understood. I believe the Bible is relevant and that a Spirit-filled preacher must be aware of the Scriptural understanding, or lack thereof, of the congregation to whom he speaks. However, this awareness is not necessary in order to make the message more palatable. It is necessary to make the message understandable.

A popular concept that has been taught for nearly twenty years is that of surveying your community and asking people what type of church they would like to have in their community. Then, the church growth experts tell us to create a church that reflects the marketing analysis and the demographics of the area. It is my firm conviction that we, as pastors and Christian workers, must survey the book of Acts, determine the type of church that Jesus desires in our community, and then go out and give that type of church to the community for God's glory.

I once heard the story of a trip taken by Mohammed Ali to the Philippines in the height of his boxing career. As he sat down on a 747 airplane, the airplane soon began to taxi and prepare for takeoff. A flight attendant walked by and noticed that Ali did not have on his seat belt. She said, "Please fasten your seat-belt, sir." He looked up proudly and snapped at her, "Superman don't need no seat-belt, lady!" Without hesitation, she stared at him and said, "Superman don't need no airplane. Now buckle up!"

Today's lukewarm Christian, and the average unregenerate man, is boldly telling God's men what they do and do not want in church. We need preachers who will, lovingly, challenge our generation to follow God, even when it is not convenient to their flesh.

Galatians 1:10 says, *"For do I now persuade men, or God? or do I seek to please men? for if I yet pleased men, I should not be the servant of Christ."* Paul knew his target audience was God Himself. He was not as concerned about pleasing men as he was about pleasing God. Paul knew that he had been entrusted with the Gospel and intended to be a faithful servant, spreading the message of Christ.

It is not the business of the church to adapt Christ to men, but men to Christ. We must never forget our calling to bring men and women to the Saviour.

The Redefining of Grace

Often, in the attempt of today's Laodicean church to please men, they have polluted the doctrine of grace. Somehow, an entire generation of Christians are being raised to believe that grace produces less holiness in the Christian life. In Titus 2:11–12, Paul wrote, *"For the grace of God that bringeth salvation hath appeared to all men, Teaching us that, denying ungodliness and worldly lusts, we should live soberly, righteously, and godly, in this present world;"* Someone who is growing in grace will not live a life that reflects less of God or His love, or a life that gives less to the work of the Lord.

In Galatians 5:13, Paul wrote, *"For, brethren, ye have been called unto liberty; only use not liberty for an occasion to the flesh, but by love serve one another."* Today, many Christians and pastors will argue that, because they are under "grace" or "liberty," they can live, seemingly, without restraints.

It is our strong conviction that someone who is under grace will find himself growing, and *"so much the more as we see the day approaching."* It is our conviction that we will not serve or give less under grace, but that we will grow under grace.

I have often heard Christians say to me, "I am under grace. I can watch R-rated movies all day long, if I want to."

"I am under grace. I can drink with my buddies if I want to."

But I have rarely heard anyone say, "I am under grace. Therefore, I am going to Africa as a missionary."

"Because I am under grace, I am giving my motor home as a part of a building offering."

This new brand of grace that is being preached in the Laodicean churches today is leading people to believe that they can live however they want to live and it is all right with God.

Even as I write this, I know there will be some who feel that we are advocating some form of harsh legalism. That is not the case at all. We are advocating true grace. True grace will lead men and women to live *"soberly, righteously and godly in this present world."*

We have no desire to see people merely conform to an outward standard, but have a strong desire to see men and women grow in the grace and knowledge of our Lord

Jesus Christ to the point that they will be conformed to His image.

May God give us pastors today who are not market-driven but Spirit-lead. May we be reminded that the church is not man's but the Lord's. Acts 20:28 says, *"Take heed therefore unto yourselves, and to all the flock, over the which the Holy Ghost hath made you overseers, to feed the church of God, which he hath purchased with his own blood."* Surely, He has purchased it with His own blood.

In Spurgeon's monthly magazine, *The Sword and the Trowel*, an anonymous article noted the tendency to drift away from sound doctrine. The author likened this drifting from truth to a downhill slope and thus labeled it the "downgrade." The inroads of modernism into the church later killed 90% of the main line denominations within a generation of Spurgeon's death. Spurgeon, once the celebrated and adored herald of the Baptist Union, was marginalized by the society and eventually withdrew his membership. His desire was simply to help avoid a downgrade. But the spirit of his age literally led to the deaths of many of the churches in England a century later. Could the same spirit in our day cause many churches to become so much like the world that one hundred years from now they will not even be noticeable as churches?

Paul's motives, in every area, were right and pure. He was not deceitful, man-centered or covetous in his ministry. There was no pretext for greed in what he was saying or doing. It was all for the glory of God.

CHAPTER FIVE

Personal Care and a Powerful Message

The second great characteristic of the church at Thessalonica was that it was a church with a personal ministry. The apostle Paul was very personal in his care of the Christians. In I Thessalonians 2:7, the Bible states: *"But we were gentle among you, even as a nurse cherisheth her children:"*

Notice that he was gentle amongst the people. We, as Bible-believing Christians, must maintain a strong position doctrinally. Our convictions will be challenged, but we must stay grounded in the Word of God. We also, however, must be gentle and easily approached, by the lost and by the new believers with whom we minister. Jude said, in verse 22, *"And of some have compassion, making a difference:"*

While preaching recently to a group of several hundred pastors and Christian workers in Australia, a man approached me during the intermission. The man's name was Wai. He told me that some of the things I had said were convicting to him. In the course of the conversation, I felt led to ask Wai if he had ever accepted Jesus Christ as his personal Saviour. As it turned out, Wai was a governmental leader from the country of Papua New Guinea. He had attended the conference with missionary Gary Keck. Gary and others had been witnessing to him and brought him to the conference with hopes that he might further understand Christianity.

I took Wai into a side office and began to share with him the love of Christ. Although he felt conviction for his sin because of a message I had preached about the Christian family, I did not condemn him for his shortcomings, sins and failures. I simply showed him the love of Christ and the way of salvation. After a few moments, Wai prayed to accept Jesus Christ as Saviour. I thank the Lord that, somehow through the message, Wai not only sensed the strength of our convictions, but also our hearts of concern for him.

This is further emphasized when Paul speaks of the necessity of being patient in the ministry. New Christians in this post-modern society need to know that, while we will not change our stand, we will lovingly nurture them where they are spiritually to help them grow in Christ.

Not only was the apostle Paul personal in his care, but he was also personal in his commitment to the people.

First Thessalonians 2:8 says, *"So being affectionately desirous of you, we were willing to have imparted unto you, not the gospel of God only, but also our own souls, because ye were dear unto us."*

People do not care how much we know until they know how much we care. Paul gave the true Gospel with an affectionate presentation. His heart and spirit were stirred within him as he visited cities like Athens that were given totally to idolatry.

A Powerful Message

The Saviour-sensitive church will not only be one with pure motives and a personalized ministry, but most importantly, it will be one with a powerful message. Thank God that there is still power in His preserved Word.

First Thessalonians 2:13 says, *"For this cause also thank we God without ceasing, because, when ye received the word of God which ye heard of us, ye received it not as the word of men, but as it is in truth, the word of God, which effectually worketh also in you that believe."* Paul clearly states that the epistle he was writing was given to him by direct revelation. This was not his opinion and these were not his ideas. This was the very Word of God. Thank God that we too can receive the Bible as the very Word of God.

First Peter 1:23 says, *"Being born again, not of corruptible seed, but of incorruptible, by the word of God, which liveth and abideth for ever."* Matthew 4:4 says, *"But*

he answered and said, It is written, Man shall not live by
bread alone, but by every word that proceedeth out of the
mouth of God."

Not only does power exist in the preserved Word
of God, but it also exists in the preached Word of God.
First Thessalonians 2:9 says, "*For ye remember, brethren,
our labour and travail: for labouring night and day, because
we would not be chargeable unto any of you, we preached
unto you the gospel of God.*" Notice Paul emphasized the
preaching of the Gospel.

First Timothy 3:16 says, "*And without controversy
great is the mystery of godliness: God was manifest in the
flesh, justified in the Spirit, seen of angels, preached unto the
Gentiles, believed on in the world, received up into glory.*"
How we thank God for the wonderful mystery of the
Gospel, which has been revealed to all men.

This is why the Holy Spirit led Paul to write Romans
1:16, "*For I am not ashamed of the gospel of Christ: for it is
the power of God unto salvation to every one that believeth;
to the Jew first, and also to the Greek.*" We must come back
to the conviction that it is the Gospel, alone, that will
draw men to the Saviour and bring true spiritual results
in the church.

Several church growth, seeker-sensitive leaders of
this generation have stated that modern-day Pharisees
are more concerned about *purity* than *people*. We are
convinced that there must be concern on both counts.
Jesus was concerned for people, but He was also concerned
about purity. Ephesians 5:27 says, "*That he might present*

it to himself a glorious church, not having spot, or wrinkle, or any such thing; but that it should be holy and without blemish."

The local church is to be the pillar and the ground of Truth. We must be concerned about doctrinal purity. At the same time, the Son of man has come to seek and to save the lost. We must continually be concerned for people. A so-called love for people that presents a message of psycho babble and diluted truth is not truly a love for people at all.

We have personally met dozens of people who are comfortable in the seeker-sensitive environment and feel accepted as people, yet have never trusted Christ as Saviour.

Recently, while helping my son purchase a car, we began speaking to the sales manager of a large Ford dealership here in southern California. He told me about the church he attends and how he loves the music and the way they "rock out." He shared with me that he felt the messages were interesting. He had attended most Sundays for the past two years. When I asked him if he knew he was on his way to Heaven eternally and had ever accepted Christ as Saviour, he said, "The thing I like about the church I attend is that they really don't pressure me into any particular decision." Can we really say that we are concerned about people when we do not confront them with their need for Christ?

Second Timothy 4:1–4 gives a charge to every true man of God. This charge states:

> *I charge thee therefore before God, and the Lord Jesus Christ, who shall judge the quick and the dead at his appearing and his kingdom; Preach the word; be instant in season, out of season; reprove, rebuke, exhort with all longsuffering and doctrine. For the time will come when they will not endure sound doctrine; but after their own lusts shall they heap to themselves teachers, having itching ears; And they shall turn away their ears from the truth, and shall be turned unto fables.*

Some of the more caustic seeker-sensitive leaders literally ridicule preaching. Advertisements have been placed in large city newspapers with a "Billy Sunday" type of figure, pointing his finger and preaching from a pulpit. The newspaper advertisement says, "If you're tired of this, come to our church this Sunday."

Now, the questions must be asked, "Have there been churches with a fundamental position that have been uncaring or have experienced some type of failure that has brought shame to the cause of Christ? Have there been caustic pulpits in our fundamental movement?" The answer is "Yes." But do we throw away the baby with the bath water? Do we stop preaching a strong, uncompromising message because of a few failures or because people simply don't like preaching anymore?

I am afraid that entertainment has hijacked many pulpits across the country. Everyone seems to want revival without prayer, preaching or consecration.

The preaching of the Word of God is an authoritative declaration of the truth of God's Word. Starving men do not need road shows in church. They need a table full of Christ.

Recently, my wife and I were out visiting folks on a Saturday morning. We were able to visit the widow of our former state senator, Pete Knight. Pete was a decorated Vietnam veteran, a test pilot, an astronaut, and later served our community in Sacramento.

After a battle with cancer, he passed away recently, so Terrie and I wanted to visit his wife and offer some encouragement and comfort to her. In the process of speaking to her in her home, she shared with us that she had a Catholic background. She said, "The one thing about the messages at your church is that they were always about Christ." I had the opportunity to ask Gayle if she knew Christ personally and if she would spend eternity in Heaven. After a few moments of sharing the Scriptures, Gayle prayed to receive Jesus Christ as Saviour.

Do we love Gayle Knight? Yes! And, because of our love for her, we could not hide the truth about Christ.

Every time we stand to preach or go out into the community with the Gospel, we run the risk of offending people. The apostle Paul not only offended people, he suffered the consequences of those offences in nearly every one of his stops along the way of his missionary journeys.

Going back to the church of Laodicea, we find one of the saddest portions of Scripture in the Bible. Revelation 3:20 tells us that Jesus is standing at the door of the church, knocking. While there may be a soulwinning application to this verse, Revelation 3:20 is speaking about Jesus standing outside the door of the church of Laodicea, wanting to come in. Unfortunately, however, the church felt that they were rich, increased with goods and did not need the Lord. They did not realize that, from God's perspective, they were poor and blind. They did not realize how desperately they needed Him. They were no longer sensitive to Him. They were merely sensitive to what they wanted and to what the people in their community wanted.

May God help us to truly consider the issues at hand today. May we recognize the necessity of being sensitive to the Saviour and be willing to stand for the Truth in this needy hour.

I pray that our church will proclaim God's Word and will reflect this renewed sensitivity to Him. May we, once again, see a true revival of repentance in our own hearts, in our churches and throughout our country.

PART THREE

A Portrait of the Saviour-Sensitive Church

by Dr. Paul Chappell

CHAPTER SIX

The Philosophy of a Saviour-Sensitive Church

For years, there has been a growing movement in our country called the Seeker-Sensitive Church Movement. Many churches, including independent Baptist churches, have been influenced by a philosophy that is very man-centered, as opposed to being God-centered. Many pastors are buying into the post-modern thought of our day and leading their churches down a path of pragmatism and carnality.

These churches are not based upon the unchanging Word of God, but are rather structured and restructured constantly to appease the appetites of men. These churches have cast off the authority of God's truth and have shouldered the mantle of designer truth, as mentioned in section one.

It has never been easy to stand and "speak the truth in love." Yet, it has never been more necessary than in the day in which we live.

> And unto the angel of the church of the Laodiceans write; These things saith the Amen, the faithful and true witness, the beginning of the creation of God; I know thy works, that thou art neither cold nor hot: I would thou wert cold or hot. So then because thou art lukewarm, and neither cold nor hot, I will spue thee out of my mouth. Because thou sayest, I am rich, and increased with goods, and have need of nothing; and knowest not that thou art wretched, and miserable, and poor, and blind, and naked: I counsel thee to buy of me gold tried in the fire, that thou mayest be rich; and white raiment, that thou mayest be clothed, and that the shame of thy nakedness do not appear; and anoint thine eyes with eyesalve, that thou mayest see. As many as I love, I rebuke and chasten: be zealous therefore, and repent. Behold, I stand at the door, and knock: if any man hear my voice, and open the door, I will come in to him, and will sup with him, and he with me. Revelation 3:14–20

Some of the saddest words in all of the Bible to me are the words, "*Behold, I stand at the door, and knock: if any man hear my voice, and open the door, I will come in to him, and will sup with him, and he with me.*" The reason these words are sad to me is because this verse tells us that Jesus Christ was literally knocking on the door of the Laodicean church–pushed out of His own church and not allowed inside!

Our goal in church ministry should always be to please Christ and to glorify Him in the church. Second Timothy 2:3–4 teaches, *"Thou therefore endure hardness, as a good soldier of Jesus Christ. No man that warreth entangleth himself with the affairs of this life; that he may please him who hath chosen him to be a soldier."* Thus, our goal is not to please a group, a denomination, or the unregenerate men and women living in our community. Our goal is not to please men or attract a crowd. Ephesians 6:6 says, *"Not with eyeservice, as menpleasers; but as the servants of Christ, doing the will of God from the heart; With good will doing service, as to the Lord, and not to men:"*

Our desire, as pastors must be first and foremost that our churches would be Saviour-sensitive in every way— giving Christ the preeminence in all things. Colossians 1:17–19, *"And he is before all things, and by him all things consist. And he is the head of the body, the church: who is the beginning, the firstborn from the dead; that in all things he might have the preeminence. For it pleased the Father that in him should all fulness dwell;"*

In this section, I want to explore with you the philosophy, the practice, and the price associated with growing a true, Saviour-sensitive church. In these chapters, we will see ten defining characteristics found in a church that places Christ at the head. Let's first explore the philosophy—the functional foundation of a church that seeks to please Christ above all.

The Ownership of the Saviour-Sensitive Church

The Seeker-Sensitive Movement has taken the authority of the church and placed it into the hands of the community at large. Pastors are taking community surveys regarding musical tastes, sermon content, service stylings, and even whether or not to use Bible words such as "sin" or "hell." Many supposed gatherings of Christians have even removed the name "church" in an attempt to blend in with the community and appeal to the lost.

Friend, the problem with this is that a Saviour-sensitive church is not "the people's church" but it truly is the Lord's church. The Bible speaks to pastors in I Peter 5 challenging them to be overseers of the flock. Yet, I Peter 5:3 says, *"Neither as being lords over God's heritage, but being ensamples to the flock."* Here we see the church is the Lord's heritage. In fact, Acts 20:28 states, *"Take heed therefore unto yourselves, and to all the flock, over the which the Holy Ghost hath made you overseers, to feed the church of God, which he hath purchased with his own blood."* The church does not belong to the people, the community, the pastor, or even the church family. The church belongs to Jesus Christ! The true, local New Testament church is an institution that Jesus Christ gave His own life to purchase unto Himself.

> *For the husband is the head of the wife, even as Christ is the head of the church: and he is the saviour of the body. Therefore as the church is subject unto Christ, so let the wives be to their*

> *own husbands in every thing. Husbands, love*
> *your wives, even as Christ also loved the church,*
> *and gave himself for it; That he might sanctify*
> *and cleanse it with the washing of water by*
> *the word, That he might present it to himself a*
> *glorious church, not having spot, or wrinkle, or*
> *any such thing; but that it should be holy and*
> *without blemish.* Ephesians 5:23–27

The very root problem in modern day church compromise is the question of authority. Christ is no longer the owner and His Word is no longer the final authority. At the heart of a Saviour-sensitive church, the pastor and the people have a deeply held understanding that Christ is the head. They submit themselves in mutual accountability and submission to the authority of His Word in all matters of faith and practice. In this kind of church, the pastor and people must die to self-will and fleshly desire and must live in constant submission to doing God's work God's way.

The Message of the Saviour-Sensitive Church

The message of the Saviour-sensitive church must always be biblical in its content. It must not merely be a message of psychology or man's thoughts with a few verses supporting what a man wants to say.

> *I charge thee therefore before God, and the Lord*
> *Jesus Christ, who shall judge the quick and the*

> dead at his appearing and his kingdom; Preach
> the word; be instant in season, out of season;
> reprove, rebuke, exhort with all longsuffering and
> doctrine. For the time will come when they will
> not endure sound doctrine; but after their own
> lusts shall they heap to themselves teachers, having
> itching ears; And they shall turn away their ears
> from the truth, and shall be turned unto fables.
> II Timothy 4:1–4

Notice the Bible says, "*For the time will come when
they will not endure sound doctrine; but after their own lusts
shall they heap to themselves teachers, having itching ears.*"
There are many teachers today who are willing to say
whatever people want to hear—whatever keeps donors
happy and airtime paid for!

The Saviour-sensitive church, however, will not
change the message to please men. At times, the message
will be confrontational. At times biblical words may
need to be defined and explained. At times the truth will
pierce and prod–bringing the sting of conviction. This
was the case when Jesus met the woman at the well in
John 4.

At Lancaster Baptist Church we have never
apologized for preaching truth that is confrontational, but
we also endeavor to make the message understandable.
For example, we define doctrinal terms from our pulpit
and illustrate with various visuals, but we will never
change the message in an effort to make it more palatable
or more tolerable—to tickle the ears. We will not remove

distasteful portions of the Scripture simply to please the society in which we live.

The Word of God is powerful and must be preached with conviction. It must be declared with authority and it must be central to every message and every Sunday school lesson. Paul said in Romans 1:14–16,

> *I am debtor both to the Greeks, and to the Barbarians; both to the wise, and to the unwise. So, as much as in me is, I am ready to preach the gospel to you that are at Rome also. For I am not ashamed of the gospel of Christ: for it is the power of God unto salvation to every one that believeth; to the Jew first, and also to the Greek.*

God said in Jeremiah 3:15, "*And I will give you pastors according to mine heart, which shall feed you with knowledge and understanding.*" Again God refers to preaching in I Corinthians 1:18–21,

> *For the preaching of the cross is to them that perish foolishness; but unto us which are saved it is the power of God. For it is written, I will destroy the wisdom of the wise, and will bring to nothing the understanding of the prudent. Where is the wise? where is the scribe? where is the disputer of this world? hath not God made foolish the wisdom of this world? For after that in the wisdom of God the world by wisdom knew not God, it pleased God by the foolishness of preaching to save them that believe.*

The message of the Saviour-sensitive church must continually lift up the cross, the Gospel of Jesus Christ, and the life-changing truth of God's Word.

The Mission of the Saviour-Sensitive Church

A Saviour-sensitive church has a two-fold mission. The first relates to the function of the Holy Spirit, and the second relates to the great commission of Jesus Christ.

First, a Saviour-sensitive church's primary goal and mission is a desire to be sensitive to the Lord in all it does. First Thessalonians 5:19 says, *"Quench not the Spirit."* A Saviour-sensitive Christian is someone who is yielded to the Holy Spirit. Titus 2:11–13 teaches, *"For the grace of God that bringeth salvation hath appeared to all men, Teaching us that, denying ungodliness and worldly lusts, we should live soberly, righteously, and godly, in this present world; Looking for that blessed hope, and the glorious appearing of the great God and our Saviour Jesus Christ;"*

A Christian, growing in the grace and knowledge of our Lord Jesus Christ, will not speak of grace and liberty as an occasion to the flesh but will realize that the grace of God is the inner working of the Holy Spirit, bringing him or her into the image of Jesus Christ.

In his book *The Disciplined of Grace*, Jerry Bridges says, "There has been a reaction to 'legalism'—but we need to watch that in our assertion of freedom, we do not give the flesh the opportunity to lead us over the precipice into sin."[1]

Many Christians in this day are so sensitive to their own perceived needs that they have given in to an accommodating style of theology in which they manipulate the Bible to say what they want rather than rightly dividing the Word of Truth. If we will be a Saviour-sensitive church, we must be sensitive to the Saviour and to the inner working of His Holy Spirit.

Second, the church must also be sensitive to the mission of the Lord Jesus Christ. In Matthew 28:19–20, Jesus was very clear when He said, "*Go ye therefore, and teach all nations, baptizing them in the name of the Father, and of the Son, and of the Holy Ghost: Teaching them to observe all things whatsoever I have commanded you: and, lo, I am with you alway, even unto the end of the world. Amen.*" Additionally, Luke 19:10 says, "*For the Son of man is come to seek and to save that which was lost.*"

The mission of Jesus Christ was to seek and to save the lost. The mission He gave us before he ascended to Heaven was to reach the whole world with the Gospel. Some churches today literally target a mere segment of the society—the yuppies, the high income earners, etc. Many seminars even teach pastors how to market their churches for a certain income level in their community.

The mission Jesus gave the church never drew such lines! The Gospel message should be taken to every single person in your community. This is what the Saviour did,

---

1. Jerry Bridges, *The Discipline of Grace* (Colorado: NavPress, 1994)

and this is what a Saviour-sensitive church will do as well!

The Motivation of the Saviour-Sensitive Church

It is obvious that the church at Laodicea was motivated by its own selfish desires. They were the church "of the Laodiceans." This church left Jesus outside, standing at the door, wanting to come in. What should motivate the church that is seeking to be sensitive to the Saviour?

The first motivation must be the Word of God. The Scriptures teach that the local church is to be the pillar and the ground of truth. First Timothy 3:15 says, *"But if I tarry long, that thou mayest know how thou oughtest to behave thyself in the house of God, which is the church of the living God, the pillar and ground of the truth."*

A Saviour-sensitive church will be strongly motivated to protect and keep the Word of God—to lift it up, proclaim it, live it, preach it, and honor it. The Word of God will serve as the final authority—the framework of doctrine and the glue of common belief that holds the church family together in faith.

Secondly, a Saviour-sensitive church must be motivated by the love of Christ. Second Corinthians 5:14 says, *"For the love of Christ constraineth us; because we thus judge, that if one died for all, then were all dead:"* It is my prayer that not one person in our church would serve in a class, the choir, or any other ministry because of a mere sense of obligation. The overwhelming force constraining us to serve Christ must simply be the fact that we love Christ and want to serve Him.

The third motivation in a Saviour-sensitive church is the grace of God. Grace is a disposition created by the Holy Spirit of God. There are at least fifteen ways that we are motivated by the grace of God and through the Holy Spirit. We are motivated to serve God and one another, *"For, brethren, ye have been called unto liberty; only use not liberty for an occasion to the flesh, but by love serve one another"* (Galatians 5:13). We are motivated to encourage one another, *"Let no corrupt communication proceed out of your mouth, but that which is good to the use of edifying, that it may minister grace unto the hearers"* (Ephesians 4:29). We are motivated to give, *"Insomuch that we desired Titus, that as he had begun, so he would also finish in you the same grace also. Therefore, as ye abound in every thing, in faith, and utterance, and knowledge, and in all diligence, and in your love to us, see that ye abound in this grace also"* (II Corinthians 8:6-7).

The grace of God at work in our hearts will do more to help us stay faithful to Christ than any other thing! Man-made "guilt trips," sensational dramas or films, high-power marketing ploys, and promotional gimmicks can never create within a church family the kind of love, devotion, commitment, and service that the incredible grace of God can produce!

CHAPTER SEVEN

The Practice of a Saviour-Sensitive Church

What does a Saviour-sensitive church look like, practically speaking? In a day when almost anything goes in the name of God and religion and when you can find "Burger King: have it your way" Christianity in every city, what does a true Bible-based church look like?

Interestingly, there are three major visible areas that seem to slip first in most "seeker-sensitive" churches. It seems that no matter the denomination or locale, the "seeker-sensitive" church movement is following the world as closely as possible in three major areas—the music, the youth, and the methods.

Let's take a close look at these three areas and what God teaches about His design and desire for the local church.

The Music of the Saviour-Sensitive Church

Time and space do not permit lengthy discussions about music in this text. The conscience of a Saviour-sensitive Christian—a Holy Spirit led believer—will bear witness against the CCM movement and will prod the believer to find a church that does not seek to conform to this world.

Needless to say, the Scriptures teach us that we are to worship with psalms, hymns, and spiritual songs. Ephesians 5:18–20 is one of several passage that teaches this, *"And be not drunk with wine, wherein is excess; but be filled with the Spirit; Speaking to yourselves in psalms and hymns and spiritual songs, singing and making melody in your heart to the Lord; Giving thanks always for all things unto God and the Father in the name of our Lord Jesus Christ;"*

The music in a Saviour-sensitive church does not focus on the musician. For eighteen years I have stated: "I do not want singers in our church who sing about the untold millions and yet never tell one person about Jesus Christ." We need musicians who truly live the Christian life and are not merely involved in entertainment.

Much of the pop-culture music of our day focuses strictly on the musician as an entertainer, and this philosophy has crept into seeker-sensitive churches as well.

Furthermore, the music in a Saviour-sensitive church does not focus on what the people want to hear or what the unsaved man wants to hear. Again, the focal point of our worship is the Lord Jesus Christ, Himself. Many churches have become so "market" or "culture" driven that they are now adapting to any and all kinds of music in an effort to "reach the world." This philosophy completely neglects the inherent power of music without words to evoke a godly or an ungodly response in the heart of a believer.

In recent days, a few authors of well-known books have stated that music is "amoral." I believe, however, that certain types of music most certainly appeal to the flesh and will draw men away from a godly and spiritual desire to worship the Lord. The term "spiritual songs" is from the Greek word *pneumatikos* which helps us realize that this is Holy Spirit given music. It cannot appeal to the flesh and to the Holy Spirit at the same time.

Music is not amoral. Every style of music without words provokes a spiritual response either toward or away from God. We cannot expect spiritual fruit to result when we bring the world's music into our church services. Churches by the thousands are incorporating carnal music into their "worship" in an effort to please men and draw crowds. Guess what? It's working! But that doesn't mean it is pleasing Christ, and it doesn't mean it's changing lives.

A Saviour-sensitive church must not be afraid of being perceived as a church with a different or traditional worship style. We must remember the words of Jeremiah the prophet in Jeremiah 10:2, *"Thus saith the LORD,*

Learn not the way of the heathen, and be not dismayed at the signs of heaven; for the heathen are dismayed at them."

Conforming to the world—musically or any other way—is the quickest way to "not reach the world." Why should the world want Christ, if Christ is no different from the world?

The music of a Saviour-sensitive church will always draw the hearts of both saved and lost men away from the world and toward the Saviour. It's that simple. In many churches, the drum set, the band, the performers simply mimic the world—and that rather poorly! The world doesn't need a cheaply reproduced late night talk show on Sunday morning. The world needs to see Christ, high and lifted up—holy!

In an effort to attract people with ungodly music, we distance them from God and defile His church with carnality. Spirit-led, Spirit-filled music will always be greatly different from the world and will in no way mimic or reproduce a secular style or feel. It will minister grace to the heart and draw the lost to new life in Christ!

> *I waited patiently for the LORD; and he inclined unto me, and heard my cry. He brought me up also out of an horrible pit, out of the miry clay, and set my feet upon a rock, and established my goings. And he hath put a new song in my mouth, even praise unto our God: many shall see it, and fear, and shall trust in the LORD. Psalms 40:1–3*

> *I beseech you therefore, brethren, by the mercies of God, that ye present your bodies a living sacrifice, holy, acceptable unto God, which is your reasonable service. And be not conformed to this world: but be ye transformed by the renewing of your mind, that ye may prove what is that good, and acceptable, and perfect, will of God.*
> Romans 12:1–2

The Methods of the Saviour-Sensitive Church

It is important to remember the phrase, "What we win them with is what we must keep them with." The methodology of the church should be biblically sound. Our message should be in agreement with the Scriptures and, in fact, they should come from the Scriptures. This is why at Lancaster Baptist Church, we still go out into the community and knock on doors, support missionaries, have special offerings, have godly women teaching the younger women, etc. Our methods are Bible-based and we must continue doing our best to follow God's blueprint (the Bible) as we serve Him.

As a side note, there are many good, sound, fundamental churches that will use slightly differing methods, yet they are methods that still fit within a biblical context. We must not be the type of insecure people who criticize a good, solid, fundamental church that may do some things a little differently (e.g. midweek service on a different night, or a building that has a different architectural style, etc.).

As long as someone holds to sound doctrine and is endeavoring to win the lost to Jesus Christ, our spirit should be to praise God for souls that are being saved here at Lancaster Baptist as well as in other ministries.

The Youth of the Saviour-Sensitive Church

One of my greatest concerns for teenagers growing up in the Seeker-Sensitive Movement is that they are seeing a watered-down concept of what Christianity truly is. They are watching their churches change before their very eyes. They see their pastors removing the pulpits and sitting on stools, removing the choirs and implementing "wanna-be" rock bands. The teenagers, in many cases, are following this example, and thus Christianity gets farther and farther from what it truly was in the New Testament.

Further, I am concerned that teenagers growing up in these types of churches will get the idea that church is about them and not about the Lord. I am convinced that many of the churches that are now joining together and emphasizing the seeker-sensitive philosophy will find that their young people will not be called to preach or to go to the mission field. They will not be attending Bible college, and many of the Bible colleges who fellowship with seeker-sensitive churches will change more and more to a liberal arts programs, as they seek to accommodate the very churches that fed them with students.

If these children are growing up in a seeker-sensitive environment, where church is all about "them," why would they consider "abandoning self" or "dying to self?" Why would they want to take up their cross and truly follow Christ?

Conversely, teenagers in the Saviour-sensitive church will see godly mentors. Philippians 4:9 says, *"Those things, which ye have both learned, and received, and heard, and seen in me, do: and the God of peace shall be with you."* We need mentors who will be able to say, "Do what you see in me." We need teenagers who will have youth pastors who emphasize a godly and holy lifestyle, who show them how to win others to Christ, and who model a faithful, separated life in the ministry.

I thank God for our youth pastors who are tremendous mentors for our young people. I believe it is because of the parents of our church, who have cooperated with our youth pastors, that many of our young people are serving God with their lives—both in and out of full-time ministry.

The Cost of a Saviour-Sensitive Ministry

There will always be a cost in maintaining a Saviour-sensitive ministry. Some Christians, who are part of the Laodicean seeker movement, will claim that a church which stays doctrinally and practically in the position which they once held, is one that does not emphasize grace. They will claim that we are legalistic or that we emphasize doctrine over the needs of the people.

A mature believer realizes that "standards" should never be the ultimate goal of a church. Jesus Christ is our goal. If we have a "standard" that is based on a Bible principle and it has helped us in living the Christian life, then we have liberty to worship the Lord in that context.

Others will justify the path they have chosen by criticizing a church that will remain the same. This is a part of the cost of being a Saviour-sensitive ministry.

Not only will the seeker-sensitive type of Christians reject the philosophy of churches across America that are more conservative, but sometimes the things stated about more conservative churches will be less than kind. While the seeker-sensitive crowd may speak about grace, they often will show very little grace when speaking of Saviour-sensitive churches.

They often remind me of the politically liberal crowd in America who speak about tolerance but are very intolerant toward the religious right. So, the seeker-sensitive movement speaks about grace but shows little toward churches that choose to worship the Lord in a "more conservative" context.

In Ernest Pickering's booklet *Are Fundamentalists Legalists?* we read,

> As we have seen, grace not only liberates
> from sin and its consequences, it also enslaves

us to Christ and produces holiness of life. As believers, we must not only celebrate the liberation of grace, but also the purification of grace. The same grace which sets us free, also challenges us with high standards of living and, thankfully, enables us to reach them. *"Brethren, the grace of our Lord Jesus Christ be with your spirit."* (Galatians 6:18)[1]

Someone who is not interested in the purifying effects of grace, which causes us to serve the Lord more faithfully, may reject a Christian who is endeavoring to grow in grace biblically. Galatians 5:13 says, *"For, brethren, ye have been called unto liberty; only use not liberty for an occasion to the flesh, but by love serve one another."* May we allow the grace of God and the liberty He has given us to motivate us to serve our Lord Jesus Christ and one another.

The Alternative to Saviour-Sensitive Ministry

As I have mentioned previously, the alternative to seeking to please the Saviour is to seek to please the culture around us. Romans 12:1–2 says,

> *I beseech you therefore, brethren, by the mercies of God, that ye present your bodies a living sacrifice, holy, acceptable unto God, which is your reasonable service. And be not conformed to this*

---

1. Enest Pickering, *Are Fundamentalists Legalists?* (Alabama: Baptist World Mission)

> *world: but be ye transformed by the renewing of*
> *your mind, that ye may prove what is that good,*
> *and acceptable, and perfect, will of God.*

We must not desire to conform to the world's system but to maintain our stand as a distinctive Baptist church.

Frankly, one may wonder where the compromise will end. If churches and pastors continue to follow the pathway of post-modernism, if they continue to question and change the truth with their new philosophies, I am afraid to contemplate what "church" will look like twenty years from now. Already, many main-line denominations ordain homosexuals as pastors. Where will the seeker-sensitive concept stop?

The Reward of the Saviour-Sensitive Church

Finally, I want you to contemplate the reward of being faithful to the Saviour. The reward will be spiritual fruit. I believe that in our Bible-preaching churches across America in which the Gospel is preached faithfully, and men and women are called upon to turn to the Lord Jesus Christ for salvation, the fruit will truly be fruit brought about by the inner working of the Holy Spirit.

Not only do I believe that we will see fruit in the realm of souls being saved, but I also believe there will be eternal rewards for churches and Christians who remain faithful. In I Corinthians 3:11–15, the Scriptures say,

> *For other foundation can no man lay than that is laid, which is Jesus Christ. Now if any man build upon this foundation gold, silver, precious*

stones, wood, hay, stubble; Every man's work shall be made manifest: for the day shall declare it, because it shall be revealed by fire; and the fire shall try every man's work of what sort it is. If any man's work abide which he hath built thereupon, he shall receive a reward. If any man's work shall be burned, he shall suffer loss: but he himself shall be saved; yet so as by fire.

Much of what is being done today, in an effort to please men, will burn as wood, hay and stubble at the Judgment (Bema) Seat of Jesus Christ.

We may not always receive the rewards and appreciation we feel we deserve here on earth, but I truly believe the goal of the Saviour-sensitive church is, and should always be, that we would hear the Lord say, "Well done, thou good and faithful servant!"